Welcome Visitors to the town of **Sumpkinville**. In this guide you will find everything you ever wanted to know, about the town, the places, and of course all the places you should go.

Sumpkinville's Oldest Attraction
Sponsored by the Sumpkinville Historical Society

Many years before you and me, the moon gave to the earth only one seed. That seed grew into Sumpkinville's magical Looking Glass Tree.

The trees Flective Orbs absorb the light from the moon to create Fogquid. Fogquid is a magic mist that surrounds the tree; some folks believe that all the magic in Sumpkinville comes from this tree.

At night, the town folk gather to see the moonlight it mimics with its leaves, and some people say that the moonlight from this tree is the most beautiful thing they have ever seen.

The entrance of the Jakel forest is where you will find this tree, and there is no fee. The Flective Orb absorption process starts at sunset but get there early if you want to get a good seat.

The most popular place in Sumpkiville is the pumpkin patch. You see its run by the greatest wizard of all, Sir. Pepper.

For hundreds of years he has been growing magical pumpkins, and once a pumpkin is grown it simply waits for its special child to come.

No one knows just how these things are done but we are pretty sure it has something to do with his powerful wand.

Sir. Peppers great, great, great, great Grandma Kinny said that she was given the wand by a powerful sorcerer named Senor Kalabaza.

She then gave the wand to Kitty Kader, who then gave it to Keyora, who gave it to Kellpee who gave it to Sir Pepper.

Did you know that Sir Pepper is the first wizard to have the wand whose name didn't start with the letter K?

Pumpkins are not born naughty, but a neglected pumpkin can mean BIG trouble, just ask Samuel.

So it's important to follow the tips listed below:

- Show your pumpkin how to behave by being a good example
- Give your pumpkin Pappy Pumpkin Pellets when it's good.
- Walk your pumpkin after dinner
- Teach your pumpkin manners (NO FARTING AT THE TABLE)
- Take your pumpkin to the DR. so it won't get the PLU

 The pumpkin patch opens daily at 5 PM, pumpkins cost $19.99 each.

There is also a pumpkin carving contest, that's where kids take non magical pumpkins and try to make them look like people.

BOOTIQUE

At the Bootique children don't buy a costume to wear they are transformed into their costume. This process, until just recently was another Sumpkinville mystery. However, Mr. Fantasma Ghostaboo the owner of the Bootique opened his workshop to the public and revealed his great machine.

The **COST-FORM-NATOR GT,** this high-tech machine changes everything you thought you knew about Halloween.

The most common question visitors ask is how to change their kids back. Do not worry we have the answers for you. To transform back you must use the Da-Fizzy-Nator shampoo which is also sold at the Bootique. Apply generously while in a warm bubble bath. This shampoo comes in three flavors watermelon, candy corn and pumpkin.

The number one costume at the Bootique is the skeleton, and Mr. Vladimir the principal at the V.V.A, is not a big fan of the vampire costume but no one knows why.

Spoogetti &

Peace, love and meatballs

It's run by Mr. and Mrs. Cooksalot, but thankfully Mrs. Cooksalot doesn't cook a lot. Rumor has it that she forgets what she is cooking and gets the ingredients confused. For example she often confuses Troll Bogies for Troll Dandruff.

The most popular item on the menu is the Meaty Beasty Balls, but beware if you don't eat them quick enough they will eat you!!!

Meatballs

makes the grooviest restaurant around.

KIDS EAT FREE ON FRIDAYS USE THIS COUPON

The best place in Sumpkinville for visitors to find yummy treats to eat, is the Candy Store. Its run by three sister witches.

Their names are Violet, Pumpkin and Raspberry.

Violet is the oldest of the three. She is so old that she has lost all of her teeth and instead of dentures she has candy corn teeth.

Pumpkin is the second oldest, and although no one agrees, she thinks she is really funny.

Pumpkin is always writing poems and telling jokes that she performs every Thursday.

Raspberry is the baby sister and she is also the one that people hardly ever see. You see Raspberry doesn't like to talk, well to people that is. Her best friend is her cat RAZ.

Rumor has it that just last week Raspberry climbed The Looking Glass tree and was meowing a song while sitting at the top of the tree. It really was a freighting scene the Sumpkinville Fire Department had to come to get her down from the tree.

Recommendations

Skelopop is the number one selling candy in the sore. One piece of this potent pumpkin flavored candy, and suddenly you are so flexible that your toes can tickle your nose.

Mucshok Chocolate Candy is another must have. This candy makes you really strong, but not for very long. After 20 minutes you return to your normal strength.

Wunchbarz are REALLY sweet they are infused with a special chirpy raspberry filling. Children will want to wiggle and giggle all day long when they eat these tasty treats.

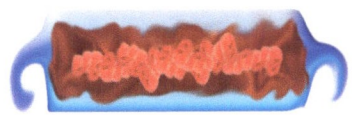

Toothy Tuesday

If you are lucky enough to have lost your tooth on Monday bring it to the store on Tuesday for a FREE piece of Taffy.

Farty Freightday

It's a party day!!! Get yourself a Skelopop and come and join us doing the LIMBO.

Taffy Thursday

Every Thursday enjoy a special poetry reading from Pumpkin.

Roses are Red
Pumpkins are Orange
I think this pumpkin
should have horns
PUMPKIN

Cathy's Cauldron

If you are looking for something delicious to drink, there is no place better than Cathy's Cauldron. Her potions are out of this world.

You should be warned though, recently The Grumbling Ogre, a very reliable source for local news, published an article about Cathy's Cauldron.

The article was written by Crusty Blackthorn. Crusty reported that Sumpkinville citizens were concerned about possible health regulations being violated at the Cauldron. One citizen was quoted saying "Cathy is a spider, hello that cannot be hygienic"

Crusty also reported that Cathy wasn't always a spider. Apparently, many years before she came to Sumpkinville, Cathy was just an ordinary girl.

The story says that while she was experimenting with potions something went very wrong and POOF just like that Cathy became a spider.

Shortly after the article was published, an anonymous caller called The Grumbling Ogre. They stated that they knew for a fact, that Cathy was turned into a spider by a great sorcerer name Smidgeon McGiggles. According to the anonymous caller, Cathy was trying to steal potion recipes from the sorcerer.

ONE EYED INN

Visitors panic when they stop by, the inn with only one eye, and wonder why the inn has only one eye. Truth be told we have no idea why, it's just the way it has always been.

While away visitors need a place to lay their sleepy heads, and the One Eyed Inn has four rooms to choose from.

Pool Room- This room includes a slime pool, a chocolate milk pool with miniature floating chocolate boats and a shower that quenches your thirst while cleaning you. The most popular flavored shower is the Bumpkin Vakneela Shockolate.

Boring Room- Trust me they mean BORING there is nothing in this room, but for some reason it is the most expensive room at the inn. Who knew that boring would be so expensive. Sumpkinville V.I.P.'S are known for booking this room for weekend retreats.

Candy Room- Complete with chocolate walls, a cotton candy bed and a cooler filled with unlimited frozen treats. This room is sure to be a dream come true for any kid! Parents should be warned though if your kid drools this room may not be a good fit. Drooling kids just don't mix well with cotton candy beds.

Mighty Unicorn Room- Here guests are inspired to always reach for the stars! The ceiling of this room is the opening to the Galaxy Boundless, it is named that because a child's potential is boundless. Guest staying in this room must wear protective headgear while sleeping, shooting stars can be painful when they hit you in the head.

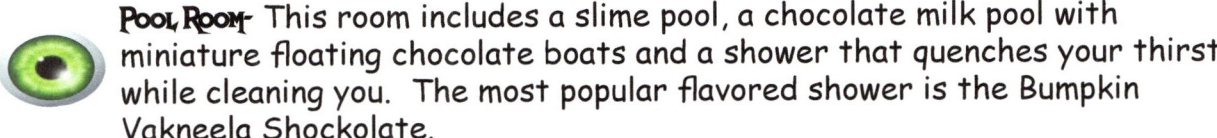

Don't forget to sign up for your free Ojo rewards card

Contributing Authors

Milton Elementary School

Nick Cantu

Nick Cantu is 8 years old and he aspires to be a scientist when he grows up. Nick is an intelligent, kindhearted and outgoing child. He is also an avid reader and loves to play basketball with his team, Brotherhood.

William Palumbo

William Joseph Palumbo III is a 9 year old student at C.L. Milton Elementary. He is an active and lively 3rd grader who enjoys school as much as playing sports. He is often described as having a kind heart and good natured personality. William has high aspirations for the future and works hard to achieve his goals.

Sofia Alcala

Sofia Itzel Alcalá is 8 years old and has dreams of being a doctor when she grows up. She is a very outgoing, cooperative, and spontaneous person. Sofia loves to go outside to run, play, and draw. She also enjoys to read, write, and do math. She also likes to sing and dance and is a kind, responsible, and caring. Sofia is a natural born leader who will accomplish many great things!

Sanchez-Ochoa Elementary School

Jennifer Hernandez

Jennifer Alexa Hernandez, a 10 year old 4th grader at Sanchez-Ochoa Elementary. Jennifer wants to help other kids learn. She enjoys spending time with her family and friends.

Juliette Zuniga

My Name is Juliette Victoria Zuniga and I am 10 yrs. old. I am in the 4th grade at Sanchez Ochoa Elementary. When I grow up I want to be a veterinarian. I want to take care of all types of animals. My hobbies include being on the school dance team, watching movies on Netflix, going camping with my family and swimming.

Marcos Ordonez

Marcos Eduardo Ordonez is a loving big brother. He is dedicated and always friendly to everyone and is always fun to be around. Even though Marcos is only 10 years old he has his mind made up that he will one day become one of the greatest athletes EVER!

Diego Marines

Diego Alonso Marines, is a 10 year old 4th grader at Sanchez-Ochoa Elementary. He enjoys working with paper and making creative things. Diego enjoys being outside, raising animals and showing them at the county fairs. He wants to be an engineer in the future.

Honore Ugarde Elementary School

Hector Bernal

My name is Hector Bernal I'm 9 years old. I love to play football with my brothers and dad. My favorite school subject is reading. I really like to write in my journal and use my imagination. I want to be a U.S Marine when I grow up and serve my country.

Juan Avina

Juan Adrian Aviña Jr. is 7 years old and hopes to one day become a professional basketball player. He is actively involved in different sports which include basketball, baseball, and swimming. He loves to read and enjoys spending time with his loved ones.

Emmanuel Lopez

Emmanuel is an extraordinary 9 year old boy that deeply cares about others. He enjoys traveling with family and going to church on Sundays. Aside from excelling in the Gifted and Talented Program; he is actively involved in his school's sports teams. Emmanuel would like to be a NBA player when he grows up.

Marcos Hernandez

Marcos A. Hernandez is 10 years old and has aspirations of being a doctor when he grows up. He likes school and likes to play chess and soccer.

Honore Ugarde Elementary School

Layla Gutierrez

Layla Gutierrez is a Star Wars fan who has dreams of becoming a famous rock star. She is a fun loving, imaginative person who loves to read comic books and making up her own jokes.

Leah Garibay

Leah Garibay is 11 years old and has aspirations of owning her own business when she grows up. She is a curious, loving and outgoing girl who loves to read, dance and make slime. She also enjoys spending time with her family and playing board games.

Alejandro Vela

Alejandro Vela is 11 years old. He is a member of the National Honor Society, Honor Choir and he enjoys helping in the community. Alejandro studies Martial Arts after school, likes to play basketball with his father and watch movies as a family.

MELVA BARRIOS

Melva Valeria Barrios was born on August 1, 2011. She is a 1st grader at Ligarde Elementary School and enjoys reading books and learning new things each day. Melvita, as she is called by family and friends, loves to dance. She adores being around her family and playing with her three siblings.

Alezzandra Lozano

Alezzandra Itzel Lozano is a 6 year old who has inspirations to become a teacher when she grows up. She is a loving, dedicated, and charming little girl who loves to read, draw, and dance.

Lorena Serna

Lorena Anaid Serna is a ten year old girl that aspires to be a doctor when she grows up. She is a caring and outgoing girl that has a passion for dancing and reading.

Please visit our website
WWW.CSBINNOVATIONS.COM.

www.ingramcontent.com/pod-product-compliance
Lightning Source LLC
Chambersburg PA
CBHW041437010526
44118CB00002B/106